## DEDICATION

*I dedicate this writing to my wonderful family and readers I love dearly.  May the Lord Jesus give you His peace.*

*I pray that you will enjoy this inspirational writing. Look for the Kindle ™ version.*

## Visit:

# GWANDINE.com

*Live, love, laugh, lament, and luxuriate in literature!™*

*Powerful Kingdom Women Series*

*Make Jesus Your Husband First!*

*Story and cover artwork by*

# GWANDINE

*FAITHFUL AND HOLY IS HE!*
*STUDIOS AND PRODUCTIONS*

ISBN-13: 978-0615843308

ISBN-10: 0615843301

## ACKNOWLEDGMENTS

*I acknowledge that Jesus Christ is Lord of all. This book design and graphics are woven from the facet of my God-given creativity.*

# What's in a Name?

Sometimes, people ask the meaning of my name, Gwandine. My mother told me that my grandmother entreated her to name me Gwandine. The meaning is listed below and accurately describes me.

*Gwandine*

*Likes to have a fun time and a good laugh*
*Charming, romantic, and expressive*
*Is very gifted*
*Takes the oppressed to heart*
*Trusting-yet wise in all she does*
*A lady whose voice is music to the ears*
*Modest, noble, clever, and adroit*
*Is thrifty, determined, and a deep thinker*

A good name is rather to be chosen than great riches, and loving favour rather than silver and gold. Proverbs 22:1

# POWERFUL KINGDOM WOMEN

Anna, a prophetess was an aged woman who had a husband for seven years since her virginity. Afterwards, she was a widow for 84 years serving the Lord in the temple of God.

She led others to the Lord for redemption. This woman had faithfully dedicated her entire life to the Lord. She could have remarried because when her husband expired, she was free to remarry. Anna was also a young woman during this timeframe.

Her life was an exemplary example of completely surrendering to the Lord. She loved God to the point where her chief concern was the redemption of Israel. She fasted and prayed for the children of Israel day and night without fail and chose to deny herself of fleshly gratification by yielding her entire life toward servitude to God. Anna was recorded by Luke in Chapter 2:36-38.

During my earlier days of salvation through Jesus Christ, it was impressed upon me that I must marry immediately or I was out of place in the church setting. I was a young woman during that time and did not understand why so much pressure was placed upon getting married right after you received salvation.

My observation led me to see many young women marry and divorce in truncated timeframes. It was as if they would divorce just shortly after the consummation of their marriages. After seeing such a rash of divorce in the church, it occurred to me years later, it would have been better if single women were taught to be married to Jesus first before considering marrying a man.

By making the Lord your husband first, it affords the opportunity and privilege to learn, grow, and develop to a deeper level of spiritual maturity, which leads to perfection in Christ. Yes, you can be perfect in Christ!

*Be ye therefore perfect, even as your Father which is in heaven is perfect. Matthew 5:48*

*Having therefore these promises, dearly beloved, let us cleanse ourselves from all filthiness of the flesh and spirit, perfecting holiness in the fear of God.* 2 Corinthians 7:1

*Finally, brethren, farewell. Be perfect, be of good comfort, be of one mind, live in peace; and the God of love and peace shall be with you.* 2 Corinthians 13:11

*Are ye so foolish? having begun in the Spirit, are ye now made perfect by the flesh? Galatians 3:3*

The reason that I included Galatians 3:3 is to make a clarification between spiritual perfection vs. fleshly perfection. Fleshly perfection is impossible; for there is nothing good in the flesh. What I mean by the flesh is the sinful lustful nature that we inherited as a result of the fall of mankind in the Garden of Eden.

*For the flesh lusteth against the Spirit, and the Spirit against the flesh: and these are contrary the one to the other: so that ye cannot do the things that ye would. Galatians 5:17*

There are those who would tell you that it is impossible to attain spiritual perfection. My past mistakes have taught me to listen and pay attention to what the Bible says as opposed to someone's comments and criticisms. Jesus would not have given us Scriptures based on the perfecting of the saints if He did not mean it. God is not a liar!

*God forbid: yea, let God be true, but every man a liar; as it is written, That thou mightest be justified in thy sayings, and mightest overcome when thou art judged. Romans 3:4*

Back to what I was talking about before: A lot of years were wasted between my walk with the Lord. People used to question me as to when was I going to get myself together so that the Lord can bless me with a husband.

Firstly, according to the Holy Scriptures, the Lord blesses men with wives. Not the other way around. Women were created for the men and we are the glory of the man. I used to hear sisters stand up and testify in church giving God thanks for blessing them with a husband. The women used to take full charge of the marriage ceremony, which is also backward.

*Whoso findeth a wife findeth a good thing, and obtaineth favour of the LORD. Proverbs 18:22*

*For a man indeed ought not to cover his head, forasmuch as he is the image and glory of God: but the woman is the glory of the man. I Corinthians 11:7*

*For the man is not of the woman; but the woman of the man. I Corinthians 11:8*

*Neither was the man created for the woman; but the woman for the man. I Corinthians 11:9*

According to the Bible, the marriage is for the bridegroom; not vice versa. Marriage is meant to be a type, shadow, and reflection of

Christ's marriage to the church (the body of believers).

Jesus Christ is our bridegroom and His bride (the body of believers) is required to make ourselves ready for His return that we may participate in the marriage supper of the Lamb.

Those that are single should seriously take this time to consider drawing close to Jesus as possible and make Him their husband by delighting in Him, rejoicing in Him, and pursuing after Him the way you would pursue after a man that you are interested in. This is a time to focus solely on Jesus and make Him the center of your joy. Allow Jesus to put a smile on your face and anoint you with the oil of gladness.

I can speak from experience. Having a husband is not going to make you happy. True fulfillment, happiness, contentment, peace, and joy come only through a real sought after sacrificial relationship with Jesus. The fantasy world of having a husband that you have probably read about in books, watched on television, or heard some woman lying and exaggerating is not real.

Your husband-to-be will put his best foot forward; meaning he will do his utmost to get you and once he knows he has you, things will change. You will wonder what happened to all of the romance, dinners, and roses. A man is not going to have you on his mind twenty-four hours a day seven days a week. Only Jesus will. A man may be concerned about hunting, fishing, or other things and you may not be in his plans.

It has been my heartfelt experience that if I could plead with women to put Jesus first in their lives, I would. I have suffered heartbreak and disappointment after disappointment trying to find something in a fleshly human being that cannot be found.

Sisters, I am here to let you know that no one will love you like King Jesus. He will be your true knight in shining armour at all times – not out of convenience or pure selfishness. Only Jesus will love you no matter how you look, what you weigh, the color of your skin, the texture or length of your hair, when you smell good, when you smell bad, when you look bad, when you feel bad—I think you get the point.

If you latch on to Jesus and learn to make Him your husband first and open yourself to love Him in addition to receiving His love, you will experience true love. You will experience joy that words cannot describe. Jesus will touch your spirit in a way that is indescribable. I know what I am talking about or in this case (writing about).

When I let go of trying to please flesh and started seeking to please Jesus and delighting myself in Him, I found myself crying tears of joy. Sometimes, I could just kick myself so-to-speak because of the years wasted.

I suffered heartbreak in my marriage like never before in life. My husband used to flirt seemingly to me after anyone that was a female (no matter how she looked). There were times when I would show him apparel at a clothing store and question his opinion and he would act as if he did not care. However, if another woman wore something he liked, he would shout it from the rooftop so-to-speak. My heart would nearly drop. My self-esteem withered.

Had I made pursuing Jesus my first choice as opposed to pursuing a husband to fulfill my longing, I would not have suffered such pain and disappointment because Jesus would have filled those voids in my life.

There is no one like the Lord Jesus. No I am not trying to sell Christ. I will admonish you that if you do not completely yield to Him, you will never know what you are missing.

No one but Jesus can fill the emptiness in your life – even if they tried.

It is impossible for anyone to love you like Jesus. A new home, car, clothing, material gain, wealth, blossoming career, baby, pet, and you name it – fill in the blank, will not make you feel like Jesus can. He will speak peace to your heart, provide you with spiritual warmth to sooth your soul, and touch you in ways that no one can.

I know that you (the reader) will find this difficult to believe. One day, I felt the presence of the Lord so strong to the point that His spirit embraced His loving arms around me as I stood in amazement. I felt His presence like never before in life and there have been many times when Jesus has touched me.

He wakes me up with a song in the morning in my spirit. His presence is ever before me. My beloved is mine and I am His as it is written in *Song of Songs* in the Bible. Man has titled it: *Song of Solomon*. However, this was written to show the love that Jesus has for his bride (the believers) and it is really titled *Song of Songs*.

No one can pick you up like King Jesus when you are feeling low. When you fall in love with Jesus, you may find yourself blowing kisses to Him.  I know I have.  You may find yourself singing to Him and He will speak to you sometimes in a still quiet voice, sometime through His Holy Scriptures, sometimes through other written communication, through people, and other means.  Jesus will <u>never</u> and I underscore this for a reason; He will never say nor do anything different from what is written in the Holy Scriptures.

*Do not err, my beloved brethren. James 1:16*

I cannot say enough about King Jesus.  He is more than amazing.  Jesus is the Preeminence of everyone and everything that exists; for He is:

I am

God

Holy

King of kings

The Rock

Almighty

The Christ

Messiah

Yeshua

Bread of life

Word of life

Resurrection

High priest

Well spring

The living water

Faithful and true

Faithful and holy

Chief cornerstone

Alpha and Omega

Beginning and the end

First and the Last

Wonderful Counselor

The Mighty God

The Everlasting Father

The Prince of Peace

The Cradle of Civilization

The Air we breathe

The Facilitator

The Organizer

Healer

The Life-giver

The Quickening

Master

Deliverer

Saviour of the world

Saviour of the body

Eternal

Lover of my soul

All Powerful

Without beginning nor end

Still small voice

First Surgeon

Creator

Creator of Man

Lamb of God

Good Shepherd

The Light

Bright and morning Star

The way the truth and the life

Anointed One

Redeemer

Immanuel

Holy One

Light of the World

Day Spring

The Word

Deliverer

Son of man

Son of God

Son of the Most High

Breath of life

Living bread

Daily Bread

Voice of many waters

Lively stone

Beloved

Servant

Song of Songs

Judge

Governor of governors

Law-giver

Psychologist of psychologists

Doctor of doctors

Lawyer of lawyers

Truth-giver

General of generals

Lord of hosts

Commander in Chief

The Bridge

Sustainer

Covenant Keeper

Keeper

Orchestrator

Lover of Souls

All Wise

All Knowing

Blessed

Merciful

Generous

Let us face the truth, Jesus is indescribable for there is none like Him nor will there ever be anyone like Him.

Jesus will not take advantage of you neither abuse nor misuse you. He will comfort you and bring calmness to your spirit.

Sometimes, when dealing with a man that knows that he has won your heart, you will be taken for granted. The excitement that he once felt from the moment he first saw you will diminish completely. You can enter a room and he may not express that same excitement and exuberance – no matter how beautiful you may be.

The Lord is not like mankind. He never changes. He never sleeps nor slumbers. Jesus is always watching over His creation.

*He will not suffer thy foot to be moved: he that keepeth thee will not slumber. Psalms 121:3*

Jesus does not change. He is not wishy-washy neither moody. He remains the same. His Word remains the same. I have learned that He can be trusted. I can count on Him. Jesus will never fail nor forsake you. He will never leave me or you! I love Him, love Him, love Him! My mere words cannot express the joy and contentment He has brought in my life.

*For I am the LORD, I change not; therefore ye sons of Jacob are not consumed. Malachi 3:6*

When you have Jesus Christ as the central focus of your life, He will make your enemies be at peace with you. Your family will fall into place. I am not saying you will not experience tests and trials. That is a part of our faith being tested as we develop and grow in Christ.

Nevertheless, throughout it all, Jesus makes it worthwhile. He causes me to rejoice, laugh, and cry tears of joy. He comforts me when I weep and feel lonely. And yes, you can be married and feel lonely. I experienced this throughout the years when I tried to place expectations on a man that only God can fulfill.

I am not trying to place a damper on marriage. I am being realistic. You will not be in the kitchen preparing meals while dressed like a runway model. You may not even maintain your figure after having children. Some women do and some do not. And let us be real; gravity does prevail as the years are accomplished. What was once up will begin to droop. The eyelids no longer look youthful. Smile lines may appear and more. You may no longer maintain that hour-glass figure (if you have one).

Ladies again I admonish you to allow Jesus to take the lead in your life. Set your affections on Him. Hunger and thirst after Jesus all the days of your life whether single or married. During my earlier days of being newly saved, the Lord spoke to me while listening to a popular evangelist during that timeframe. I did not know of this woman as I had never heard of her. I just knew that she was popular and one of my cousins took me to listen to her preach.

It was as if something drowned out the sound of the evangelist and I heard the still small voice of the Lord speak to me and say, "Thirst unto me."

Jesus desired me to thirst unto Him and to pursue Him; not visiting evangelists and the cares of this world.

How I wish that I had obeyed His still small voice years ago. Jesus would speak to me throughout the years and tried to get me to pursue Him as opposed to desiring to be blessed with a career, house, husband, and more – not necessarily in that order. However, Jesus was not even on the list of my priorities – albeit I was saved!

I was baptized in Jesus' name and filled with the Holy Spirit evidenced by speaking in other tongues as the Spirit of God gave the utterance. Nevertheless, I failed to cultivate a real relationship with my Creator. I would go on three day fasts with the church for Solemn Assembly and fast during other times. Albeit, during my fast, I would always long and thirst for a husband and material things of this temporal world. It took a great heartbreak brought on by my (still-present husband and now pastor) that the Lord used to cause me to make a turn in my life to seek and pursue after God and to fall in love with Him with all of my heart and never, ever again, put anyone or anything before Him. Jesus is now most important in my life.

Without Him, life is meaningless. It is not even worth living. I now have my priorities straight. This is how much I love Jesus! I love Him with all my heart, soul, mind, and strength! I also consider my neighbor as a reminder that if I do not love my fellowman, then I do not love Christ. Therefore, I love Christ and I strongly admonish you to do likewise. You do not want years to pass by and have to learn the hard way as I did. Make Jesus your Lord and (husband first). And remember ladies, no one will ever love you the way Jesus does.

I do not care how sweet a man makes his words sound during his pursuit or conquest of you. Guard your heart because once he marries you, you may <u>never</u> hear those words he used to pursue you. You may <u>never</u> receive the special treatment that he once used to give you. If you marry a man that continues to treat you the same as he did during his pursuit of you, praise Jesus! However, do not rely on this. The devil will step in and use it as a weapon against you. If the enemy sees that you have set your affection on Jesus first and foremost, he will not have much to work with in that area. The Bible explains that the devil resists those that are steadfast in the faith.

*Whom resist steadfast in the faith, knowing that the same afflictions are accomplished in your brothers that are in the world. I Peter 5:9*

Remember, people have a tendency to change; but the Lord never changes. I could have given up. The Lord told me to follow my heart concerning my marriage. Be sure and read my next set of writings titled: *Don't Trash Your Marriage!*

You cannot go wrong making Jesus your husband first. You will be richly blessed if you choose to do so. Your experience with the Lord will be enriching and rewarding. The peaceful rewards are true blessings and nothing can be compared to having the peace of God.

Be blessed my sister in Christ and know that Jesus loves you. Wait on the Lord for Him to join you to your husband-to-be.

# ∽ CONCLUSION ∾

There are numerous powerful kingdom women in the Bible that withstood opposition to the point of risking their lives to take a stand for God.

Remember, put Jesus first and foremost in your life and know that He is your true husbandman and be a powerful kingdom woman of God. When you allow Jesus His rightful position, you are ready to handle marriage to a man.

## ∽ From the Author: ∽

All artwork, graphics, paragraph dividers, illustrations, cover design, and the internal book design are woven from my gifted hands inspired by the Lord.

# References and or Bibliographies
## *King James* Version of the *Holy Bible*
### And life experience

ও৯ ৫১

All Scriptures utilized in this book were taken from the *King James* Version of the *Holy Bible*, which is in the public domain in the United States.

Gwandine is an anointed pastor, author, artist, and mentor to young women in Christ. She has also ministered and shared her testimony to homeless individuals.

The strong anointing she possesses came as a result of her years of suffering, which she learned that Jesus is her faithful Rock.

During her youthful years, she lived in an unstable home environment nearly starving. She sometimes found sustainment by consuming outdated food discarded in garbage dumpsters, which was very unhealthy.

She suffered numerous rapes throughout her years, mental, physical, emotional, verbal abuse, and rejection by men before and after she received Christ as her Lord and Saviour. It was then that she quickly learned that Jesus never promised her that life would be easy. Nevertheless, He proved Himself faithful throughout it all. Gwandine learned that Jesus will heal your broken heart and that He makes all things new.

Visit her website at Gwandine.com. She writes Christian non-fiction and Christian parables. She has written Christian parables of encounters in the Old West, Christian mysteries, inspirational poetry, and painted oil on canvas. Gwandine is gifted to glorify God! She refuses to create works that fail to glorify Him. In times past, she wrote a couple of secular books and felt uncomfortable. The Lord convicted her heart and she repented from her dead works.

*O LORD our Lord, how excellent is thy name in all the earth!  Psalms 8:9*

If you have not received Jesus Christ as your Lord and Savior, I urge you to please do so.  We are living in the last days and times and He is soon to return for His people who are the called body of believers that have kept His Holy word.

He will forgive you from all of your sins and unrighteousness if you pray and ask Him to.  He desires to baptize you in water and with His precious Holy Spirit evidenced by speaking in tongues (languages) as the Holy Spirit gives the utterance.  The Holy Spirit empowers you to live a holy and blameless life before God.

Jesus did not say that all of your problems would suddenly disappear. He did promise never to leave nor forsake you.  Pray and seek the Lord for a Bible believing full Gospel church to fellowship with other believers for edification and spiritual enrichment. Remember that Jesus loves you and so do I. One day I heard a voice from Heaven sing these words: *Faithful and Holy is He!* After seeking the Lord for a name for my studio and publishing imprint, I chose to use *Faithful and Holy is He!* The Lord has proven Himself Faithful and Holy!

## *Faithful and Holy is He!*

## *Our blessed Lord and Saviour, JESUS CHRIST*